Prison Segmentation For Sentence Segments Design

Reverend Mike Wanner

Table Of Contents

Background 4

Introduction 5

1 - Why I am Writing This Book 6

2 - The Segmentation Effect 8

3 - Build-In Sentence Modifiers...9

4 - Many Ways to Serve a Sentence 10

5 - Judges & Angel Raphael 11

6 - Density Can Act As an Obstacle 12

7 - Fait Accompli 14

8 - Big Patio or Sidewalk Blocks 15

9 - Powerful Language Instruments 16

10 - Developing a Plan...17

11 - Prisoners In Segmentation Panels 18

12 - Correctional Officer Panels 20

13 - Administration Panels..21

14 - Legal Community Panels..22

15 - Guidelines for Participation 23

16 - Sentence Specifics to Consider.......................................24

17 - Sentence Reduction Triggering Event Goals....................25

18 - Why Compile This in Prison 26

19 - Performance Certification & Recommendation 27

20 - Recommendations to The Court 28

21 - Thank You 29

22 - Don't Worry Ever 30

23 - Resource List 31

24 - Angels Please Prayers...34

25 - Private Channeling..35

26 - Reverend Mike Wanner 37

Background

The legal process in American courts has been very complicated for a long time. There are many variables that need to be sorted through to be in compliance with the laws and respect the rights of each individual.

The administrators of our government do not have an easy job and balancing multiple priorities consumes a lot of time. Doing the job right requires diligence and tenacity.

Please consider the options suggested here as opportunities to refine the process in pursuit of efficiency, respectfulness for all participants and proper administrative oversight.

Introduction

I want to trigger mindset shifts in the prisoners as well as employees and the community. We need a lot more Objective Productive Dialogues about Enhancing the lives of Prison Employees, Prisoners, Taxpayers and the Families of Each of these groups.

I hope that this book continues the work started by my other books and continues to enhance the lives of Prison Employees, Prisoners, Taxpayers and the Families of Each of these groups?

As I have been writing my early books on the subject of Prisons, the complexity of the process has been amazing to me.

I have previously published 44 books so far about the prison situations, and they fall into the following categories:

4 *Angel Raphael Speaks Books about Prisons*
1 *Prison Jobs book*
1 *Contained Care Communities: Concept*
1 *Australia In Miniature*
5 *Prison Possibilities Dialogue Series Books*
5 *Prison Possibilities Idea Books*
1 *Prison Genius Pool: "So Much Genius In Jail."*
2 *Prisoner Family Books*
9 *Prisoner Projects (Writing, Cell Clearing, and Blessings, Prisoner Professors, Prison Reiki?, Dowsing, Solitary Community, Communications, Motivation, Real Estate)*
1 *Judges and An Angel Rule On Possibilities*
1 *Ideas For Prison Wardens*
13 *Prison Segmentation Books*

1 - Why I am Writing This Book

The United States Sentencing Commission has the vital job of considering the criteria that are used for sentencing and alternatives to sentencing.

The original 1987 Guidelines Manual provided for alternative sentencing options, and since then there have more amendments.

Despite the changes, it seems that the use of alternatives is less than optimal.

Specialized court programs have surfaced in some areas, but the development of alternatives may be mired in complexity and bureaucracy which has to be perfectly understandable because of the many variables that could be involved.

It seems to be that well-intentioned conversations get started, but then the reality of complexity becomes apparent.

Alternative Sentences courts are continuing to be useful in some places to help in problem-solving. We may also find that common sense can be available by asking the right questions to the right people at the right time.

The idea here is to look at the effects of sentencing with an eye towards creating a template that might help the courts in the future to issue sentences with variables that can enhance the likelihood of increased prison rehabilitation and expedient reentry.

Reverse Engineering could be the tool to look at the end product in order to determine the path that was taken to get to the end.

Reverse engineering is a way of looking at design information about a process or product analytically so that you can use that knowledge to select characteristics to redesign, modify, reanalyze or compare to other similar or dissimilar methods or products in exacting detail.

There could be many reasons or benefits that may enhance your database without violating copyrights in place, but care should be exercised not to use proprietary information without permission.

The analysis is proposed to be done by prisoners in prison segments to help the courts, the taxpayers. Prisoners reentry, the prisons, the prison staffs and the families of them all.

2 - The Segmentation Effect

Segmentation takes incarceration to a controlled condition of freedom from the intensity of interference that naturally flows from the congestion of too many people in too little space. The controlled separation allows possibilities for peace, tranquility, and positive outcomes.

Part of the beauty of segmentation is the ability to stabilize the experience of prisoners and allow enough pause to provide a regrouping opportunity for each participant. The treasure could be the opportunity to be safe for a while from specific stressors that are not compatible with peace of mind and or personal safety.

An individual's ability to apply for a pause from the intensity of everybody else's stress can go a long way to keep the peace and harmony of a facility. The judgment of a sentence alone may be too much for some people to process and may take them closer to the dark side of their being than they would typically go.

Just the idea that there could be options to any experience that disturbs them could allow many people to have hope that would not otherwise exist. People are fragile, and there is little value in missing no-cost opportunities that might prevent episodes of upheaval.

Personal peace in Prison can promote community tranquility and freedom from pushback on insignificant points. Segmentation can also allow efforts to create systemic change, and this book invites ideas regarding sentencing to do that without pushback.

3 - Build-In Sentence Modifiers

While I have documented the concept of prison segmentation for effective prison experience modification, I have become aware that a built-in segmentation dynamic may be just the ticket for bringing flexibility and cost containment systemically.

A significant element of segmentation is a move away from the congestion of living too close to others. Hopefully, vital aspects of segmenting sentences could have cost-cutting and quality of life enhancements.

The sentence assigned by order of the court is usually applied as a time period which only has a change element that moves the time served in one direction. Bidirectional increments could make a world of difference in the benefits and costs of incarceration.

Let us begin to plan for and adopt a strategy that embraces the individuality of prisoners and their flexibility to change and adapt to the level allowed by the rules or incarceration known as their sentence and the creativity and generosity of their spirit.

It will take considerable effort to redesign the incarceration community to allow this results enhancement range of possibilities. The value of changes like this to the residents of our prisons and the staff of those facilities could be monumental.

4 - Many Ways to Serve a Sentence

Every prison facility is different, and we may use that as an analogy for incorporating some flexibility by design into sentences. It is not unusual for time penalties to be added to extend terms for complications and/or punishments for bad behavior so that sentences of identical length may develop into different periods of time served.

We could begin to entertain the idea that penalties that increase sentences and cost could also be inverted. A way to do that would be to add structure to the initial court order (If the Court Approved) that could incorporate precise performance criteria.

Affirmative prisoner conduct could trigger reassessment so that time could be shaved off the sentence. A somewhat automatic process can trigger a standing order to be recorded without a need for a new court order.

While the concept may be hard for any court to visualize at the onset to set perspective for later truncation, we could propose here in this book some ideas that could invite proposals to suggest conditional sentence language. There could be criteria proposed from many areas of the legal community.

Administration may have values that are separate from the perspectives of correctional officers, officer's families, prisoners, prisoner's families and other facility staff. The agency that actually owns the physical facility may have different concerns altogether than those mentioned above as might contractor's, professional medical and technical staffs and others.

5 - Judges & Angel Raphael

I wrote the book *Judges and An Angel Rule On Possibilities: We Can Cut Sentences & Prison Costs* after I became alarmed when reading about the story of a Federal Judge in Nashville who quit the bench because he was required by duty to declare a mandatory sentence that he did not agree with.

As I understand things as a non-legal observer, the sentencing rules can be exacting. The law is the law, and it is specific as required by the traditions of the Judicial System. There is a precedent for the stiffness as it is required by law and laws stand until they are changed in accordance with the enabling legislation.

Laws in place set the rules for all participants. While it is not easy or quick to do, laws can be changed.

Changing law requires a dedicated analysis and careful evaluation of every aspect of every law that is pertinent to the situation that is to be replaced. Nothing can be taken for granted as laws that are changed will have a new rigidity.

It is essential that a thorough analysis of the total situation is made, so there are no surprises for anybody.

6 - Density Can Act As an Obstacle

The number of people in prison can be a big part of the complexity and rigidity in prisons. When we simplify the interpersonal dynamics, we effectively make the facility more user-friendly.

Angel Raphael channeled a message about prison rehabilitation which would be compatible with segmented sentences.

"Prison Rehabilitation

The answer to prison rehabilitation is purpose. While some institutions may have initiated programs to engage their residents, the feeling of a purposeful life brings a new reality to the incarcerated.

Purposes to consider will be ones that work for the incarcerated as well as the society which actually pays the bills. Special characteristics to include would be the creation of a feeling of accomplishment generated by prisoner effort and drastic cost savings for the institution.

The real loss to prisons is wasted time, no productivity and no graciousness of interactive genius. If invited, the right use of time can provide different results than now seen.

There is no profit to society when cruelness is applied to the control of citizens. There may be temporary security, but that comes at a big price to the potential of all.

The best way to learn about what is possible is to listen to the troubled stories of the incarcerated people. Their genius can be tapped by mining information about how to fill the gap that they slipped in to so that newer walkers on their path can find the gap filled by their charity of sharing their pain as a love patch to the sinkholes of society.

The answers through this channel are coming differently than most could conceive and that is because neither you nor I have a job whose agenda has its own needs.

You ask to imagine how much can be cut from prison costs to maintain security, improve lives, create new industry and improve the focus, flavor, and flair of American life and you dowsed for an answer. You got 47% reduction, and you questioned your dowsing. Your questioning is wise because there is a huge industry that has roots in the status quo.

While that is true, your answer has potential that will serve the ones that would resist the initiatives that flow from the message. Their positions are survivable as is for a time unknown but their openness to change can also serve their security.

The change will happen even if they choose to use their money to resist the inevitable avalanche of change. Their opportunities are paramount in the areas of personal safety for all and the possibility to create new meaningful arrangements that are self-sustaining for all levels of the resident base and those employed in the industry. ARS 10

7 - Fait Accompli

Fait Accompli is a term that has its roots in the French language and refers to something that is already accomplished and presumed irreversible.

The problem element with the concept as it refers to prison sentences is within the permanence of the decision. It can be compared to pouring concrete over the verdict.

8 - Big Patio or Sidewalk Blocks

Sentences, in many ways, are like big blocks of concrete that are created in a big chunk that can be very difficult to dislodge. Once it is down, it stays down.

A big chunk of the obstacle can stifle a life. Prisoners are like all other people in that the appearance of things weighs heavy on the ideas of possibility.

You are probably aware that sidewalks are usually made in blocks, and while they may be poured together, they are lined or defined and or separated in some way. The separations (segmentation) allows sidewalks to be split up into pieces without having to destroy the significant block of concrete.

Sidewalks can be added to like sentences. sidewalks can also be easily segmented and decreased, unlike prison sentences.

If we could find a way to make sentences as flexible as sidewalks, then we could eliminate the big block of obstacle that stifles so many prisoner's thoughts and ls.

The courts could do that by adding sentence definition with lines and definitions and separations to the degree necessary to make the sentence malleable over time to an instrument that can help uplift prisoners level of possibilities for individual self-determination.

While that may sound like an impossible assignment to impose upon the court, it could be simpler than it seems and the results could be monumental for many prisoners and cities.

9 - Powerful Language Instruments

With enough definition, the system could serve up a template of variables that could efficiently personalize sentences to be reactive to the positive efforts of each prisoner. It will be necessary to do a lot of analysis to determine the many ways that segmentation can work in sentences.

Initial documentation could prepare for the introduction later of types of efforts by a prisoner that would trigger evaluations that could further trigger referrals to reviewers who could dig deeper still and bring candidates up for continued reassessment.

Steadfastness will be needed in this process so that the process can grow roots and begin to redefine the performance expectations for prisoners and officials alike.

There is an old story about The Tortoise and the Hare, and it is referenced on Wikipedia as one of Aesops Fables. Variations of the story in folklore can give different perspectives, but for me, the interpretation is that slow and steady can win the race.

You may find in life many tricks, but you can always find power in persistence. Let us bring tenacity to the projects of sentence mitigation.

This effort can bring rehabilitation realities to purpose-driven prisoners. Powerful sentence structuring tools, increased quality of life for prisoners, ex-prisoners the families of them all and the communities they live within are also valuable byproducts.

10 - Developing a Plan

The courts have plenty to do already so it would be entirely unfair for anybody to expect them to take on this project.

A collaborative effort would make sense and prison would be an ideal place to start the discussion as there is a lot to be said for self-interest. There is also a lot that can be said about the respect that could serve everybody well.

Prisoners are smart and would realize that this process would not be like Monopoly's "Get Out Of Jail Free Card." It will take a lot of diligent effort to get any court to agree with their plan so they would be mindful from the outset, that the effort would need to be very deliberate and comprehensive.

A transparent process would serve best as would the inclusion of the suggestions from as many court clerks, lawyers, prosecutors, prisoners, correctional officers, wardens, clergy, probation officers, employers, and reentry specialists.

This process is not intended to open the doors for those who do not deserve to exit, but it is meant to offer a reasonable opportunity for people with integrity to determine that they want to change their lives and then do it.

General population efforts may work in some facilities, and I would encourage them. I also believe that a project in segmentation will have a higher likelihood of success as there may be fewer people trying to obstruct your progress.

11 - Prisoners on Segmentation Panels

Prisoners could participate in panel discussions that might provide a lot of input as to what might make common sense. People process from their own perspective and everybody's perspective could be different.

Are you one of those people who has uttered the phrase "Why didn't I think of that?" The answer well might be that the person who made the discovery is one who was impacted negatively by the status quo of the situation and that may have provided motivation.

Sensitive awareness can grow from experiences at every level of the community. Where you were born, and the priorities of those around you may well have contributed to the peace and tranquility or your awareness that some things could be better in the future, but you may need to wait until an optimal time.

Self- preservation in prison may require that you benefit from keeping your mouth shut about things that others may strongly disagree with so that you do not have troubles that could threaten the peacefulness of your present situation.

Prisoner panels for segmenting sentences could allow you and others to use ingenuity to create changes generically by offering bright ideas as some of the choices on a spectrum for the system to draw from.

The most important contribution that a prisoner panel may make could be about the kind of things that need to be built into a sentencing plan that can be embraced by prisoners so that their performance can mitigate their sentence and have everyone moving towards a smaller population base with the best cooperators getting more freedoms and or total freedom and the worst offenders being treated fairly in a facility that is the least restrictive that it needs to be.

Prisoners will know what they might be able to suggest, but they should be cautious to make reasonable suggestions that would stand the scrutiny of correctional officers, administration, and supervising prison agencies.

Prisoners could get real creative and offer suggestions that facility employees, correctional officers, and administration would not think of making.

12 - Correctional Officer Panels

It is likely that correction officers would know a lot more about prisoner's motivation than they might think they do. While it may be unlikely for workers with a family to volunteer their wisdom publicly when it has not been invited, it may be very gratifying to them to have their knowledge invited privately to a discussion with other staff and correctional officers.

The subtle sharing of stories about the correction officer observations about prisoner reactiveness may be able to isolate approaches that could prove helpful in the future. Being able to anticipate and interact positively can be very powerful in keeping the prison peaceful.

Safety awareness can be critical at times to correctional officers, and I would encourage you to think that some of that may be attainable by putting your prisoner's interests into a proper perspective that gets and deserves your support.

Giving and receiving are reciprocal and giving your attention to the highest and best good for all can be very beneficial to the self-interest of yourself and your family.

"What goes around comes around (anon.)" is a quip that expresses the idea quite nicely. Your gifts to others are like boomerangs that come right back to you.

Correctional Officers can be very pivotal to the success of this effort. Please feel free to dig deep for ideas, neutralize them so they can be processed by prisoners and share them so that can be discussed in detail and form the base for a success trigger.

13 - Administration Panels

Administration may have a strong dollar and cents component, and this is all justified by the fact that the responsibility is a fiduciary one as the administrators are handling the money of the community of taxpayers.

Of course, those same administrators have a fiduciary responsibility to the employees and contractors who serve the facility.

Administrators would be wise to balance the values of all participants in the facility.

Facility Owner agencies also have interests that can be invited to the discussion in formats that may preserve the secrecy and identity of the organization.

Administration may have a lot to offer that others might not ever think about. Try floating some precise technical ideas that could make a difference in unusual areas of expertise that are not your forte.

There are a lot of people with skills, and it may be that someone on a panel could pull out a profession and weave it into a project that gets momentum and helps the whole system.

Please open the mind to all creative options as this whole project is a mind-expanding initiative.

14 - Legal Community Panels

Prosecutors, Defendant's Lawyers, Judges, and the whole spectrum of technical skill practitioners within the legal community could also be invited to submit ideas to the Prisoners in Segmentation Panels that are designing options to be included in Segmentation Options. All potential options under the right circumstances (A Masterplan) could provide opportunities that prisoners could use to present authoritative justification for considering specific parts of skill sets as potentials to prep for service, and that can lead to freedom.

A universal institutional format for use in the measurement of individuals may be ill-suited to the task. Creating options that highlight the skills and distinct competency possibilities that one can work towards can take the whole incarceration community to a new level of potential awareness.

The evaluators for parole boards are likely accustomed to standardized presentations that speak to the ideas that are deemed as appropriate to present. That kind of display is unlikely to trigger recognition of individual creativity that can be a benefit to the whole institution.

It is probable that the panelists desiring to submit conviction segmentation option triggers for sentence truncation would want to provide as many options as possible. More options could provide truncation for more convictions and then more prisoners qualifying for sentence truncation.

15 - Guidelines for Participation

There are about 6,000 prison facilities in America, and each could easily have their own guidelines for segmentation and any activities thereof. It is Important for all participants to read and know the rules that will apply to their specific facility.

This effort would only make sense if the judicial system in your area explicitly endorsed the concept and was willing to consider your recommendations. All participants are requested to ascertain for yourselves that you are satisfied that your efforts will be in accord with the Court and you are fully aware of the application process authority and the clerk or agent of the court.

The Court rules must be explicitly followed.

16 - Sentence Specifics to Consider & Evaluate

Consider all the enabling court orders and the following values from each prisoner in the whole prison and legal communities as possible events and percentages of reduction:

Freedom from Conflict of any kind with other residents and staff.

Significant Accomplishments of all kinds.

Design Team Participation and contributions.

Educational Accomplishments.

Skill gifting to other prisoners.

Problem-solving for others.

Personal Designed Lifestyle Goals Adopted
   a. Physical Developments
   b. Emotional Developments
   c. Mental Developments
   d. Spiritual Development

17 - Sentence Reduction Triggering Event Goals

An ongoing process of evaluation would be a valuable component of this process. Panelists would submit goals suggestions they would recommend for consideration, and those goals could gather support from other panelists who want to see those items developed as segment triggers to be suggested to the court.

Goals should be SMART:

Specific by containing clearly defined outcomes.

Measurable in increments that target the specific target

Attainable within a reachable plan.

Realistic from a resources perspective

Timely events with a deadline.

Sentencing formats could be progressively reviewed to fine tune the processes, documentation, and results.

18 - Why Compile This in Prison

The whole community can participate in resetting the sentencing order suggestions to the appropriate court in order to consider the situations of the incarcerated in light of optimizing the possibility for success. Minimal incarceration with modifications that add perspective can contain common sense approaches to create practical change and create taxpayer savings.

Keeping people in prisons is very costly, and we all need some relief from the extreme taxation that results from imprisoning vast numbers of our fellow citizens.

Taxpayers in the greater community have an interest in how our tax dollars are spent. Incarceration is a considerable expense, and if there were unlimited funds in our national budget, there would be no need to consider changing anything unless some additional fairness was a prominent goal.

Unfortunately, the national budget is stretched by government expenditures, and it makes sense for us to evaluate the reasonableness of our expenses. We could find there are many opportunities for relaxation when change happens.

A byproduct of sentence segmentation might be increased awareness of the needs of the community so that alternatives to incarceration are triggered by serving the citizens in a way that stimulates individual success in law-abiding pursuits.

19 - Performance Certification & Recommendation

Approval Steps

Designation of Agency to certify, register, effect, authorize, and submit the recommendations for the reduction authorization would be needed at the appropriate level according to law and judicial orders in strict compliance with all written Orders of The Court.

Assumptions will not be helpful. Inquiries will help to prepare proper documentation and can succeed.

The process of certifying the recommendation will require:

Who - The Candidate Pre-Requisites

What - The Type of Reductions Suggested.

Where - The Prisoners will perform what.

When - The Effective Time of Application

How - The Order Will be Activated.

Why - The Order is Recommended.

20 - Recommendations to The Court

The Courts in each community can determine the level of authority and procedure for their community.

The final steps in Process will be:

1. Declaration of Appreciation To The Court.

2. Recommendation of a Comprehensive Plan to as many Specific Courts in the Community as possible.

3. The recommendation of a review process and timelines for future Court Actions and Process evaluation.

4. Request For Filing Recommendation For Sentence Truncation.

5. Clear Contact Information for the Reply.

The final compilation summary could be done different ways in different facilities.

Identification of individual contributors to the whole process could be optional. Identification of individual contributors to the summary process could also be optional but might carry more credibility with identities.

For
Considering
These
Ideas

Ever

It Does Not Help Prayer Still Does!

Resource: http://Create-A-Prayer.com

23 - Resource List

Distant Healing Sessions (or Join Mail List) – Write To mikewann@voicenet.com

Books by Rev. Mike at <u>www.Amazon.com:</u>

Veterans Healing Six Pack
1. *Trauma Healing Options for VA Hospitals: Help for Veterans to Own Their Healing and their future.*
2. *Trauma Healing Action Steps for Veterans: Help to Start Healing*
3. *Trauma Healing Action Steps for Veterans: Empowerment*
4. *Trauma Healing Action Steps for Veterans: Forgiveness*
5. *Trauma Healing Action Steps for Veterans: Thought Freedom*
6. *Tea For Veterans: Welcome One Home*

PTSD Power Pack:
1. *The PTSD Project: Turn Pain To Power*
2. *PTSD & Soul Retrieval: Putting One Back Together*
3. *PTSD & The Purple PAD: Calling all Scientists and PTSD Patients*

Angel Raphael Speaks Volume 1: Take Courage! God Has Healing in Store for You!
Angel Raphael Speaks Volume 2: Take Courage! God Has Healing in Store for You!
Angel Raphael Speaks Volume 3: Take Courage! God Has Healing in Store for You!
Angel Raphael Speaks Volume 4: Angels, Addicts, Alcoholics & Prisoners – Oh Yeah!
Angel Raphael Speaks Volume 5: Prisoners Caring for Alcoholics - Australia In Miniature Projects Intro
Angel Raphael Speaks Volume 6: Prisoners Caring for Addicts - Australia In Miniature For Addicts
Reiki Journaling from Japan
Reiki Is Alive: God's Great Gift
Four Parts to Healing
Distant Healing: We Are All Connected
Stress Release Energy Work: How To Cope

Does Reiki Love Heal Cancer?
Group Consciousness
Salute To Philadelphia VA Medical Center: Thank You
Reiki Transcript for Reiki 2 & 3 Channels: Dr. Usui Is That You?
God Bless Kindle & Amazon
Puppies Are Different From People
If Your Dog Dies
Toy Guns Are Obsolete
Great Spirit Made Children With Red Skin: AND
The Cage of Fear: Is Not Locked
God Made Children Red, Yellow, Brown, Black & White: Greet Each Child With Kindness
Emergency Medical Kindness In The Cradle Of Liberty: Big City – Cracked Bell
Angels Are Always Around Addicts and Addicts: Help Is Near Now! Invite It In!
Angels Are Always Around Addicts and Alcoholics: Volume 2 - Tools To Help Re-Light Your Life
Prison Jobs Now: Providing Care For Addicts And Addicts
Controlled Care Communities Concept
Prison Possibilities Dialogue Series: Concept
Prison Possibilities Dialogue Series: Volume 2, 3, 4, 5 Dialogues
Prison Possibilities Voluntary Exile
Prison Possibilities Corrections Coaches
Prison Possibilities For Mexicans: Is A Boat Better Than A Wall?
Prison Possibilities Family Time: A Reason to Thrive!
Prison Genius Pool: "So Much Genius In Jail."
Prison Possibilities Access Control: Prisoner Access by Request
Prisoner's Lawyers Can Save The American Economy: Make A Buck Doing It & ...
Prisoner Family Talks, Days, Stays & Vacations: Connecting Helps Healing
Prisoner Writing Projects: Write To Heal, Start Over & Reconnect
Prison Cell Clearing & Blessing: Clear Entities, Chase Ghosts, & Create Sacred Space
Prisoner Professors: Show You Are Aware Create Change With Care
Prison Reiki? Maybe Someday? A Gateway To Help Heal Prisons & America?

Judges and An Angel Rule On Possibilities: We Can Cut Sentences &
Prison Costs
Ideas For Prison Wardens: Leadership Is Not Easy
Solitary Community: Could Community Support Cut Costs and Issues?
Prison Project Communications Team: Communications Can Change
Lives
Motivating & Empowering Prisoners? Invite Prisoners To Find Their
Motivation
Prison Segmentation For Safety, And Sanity, Security, Peace, and Space
Prison Segmentation For Security
Dowsing for Prisoners; Answers from Above
Ex-Prisoner Possibilities With Real Estate Investors
Prison Segmentation For Joint Ventures
Prison Segmentation For Your Rehabilitation: R U Ready?
Prison Segmentation For Family Villages
Prison Segmentation For Senior Prisoners
Prison Segmentation For Coaching Clubs
Prison Segmentation For Miracles

Little Books on Kindle.com by Rev. Mike:
English Medical History Questionnaire For Non-English Speakers
English Language Helper For Non-English Speakers
Wise Wonderful Women Are The Well Of The Family
Answers for Test & Research: Dowsing Power
Crisis? Reiki! Baby? Reiki!
Bible References For Healing
Angel Raphael Speaks – Prisons
Angel Raphael Speaks – Veterans
The Saint Off Interstate 95

24 - Angels Please Prayers

Addict's

Angels of Healing Selected
Help Me to Stay Directed
Come To Me From The Sky
I Am Ready to Succeed Not Try
If I Don't Invite You In
I Might Not Win
I Have Been Lost For Too Long
Help Me To Stay Strong

&

Alcoholic's

Angels of Healing On High
Help Me to Stay Dry
Come To Me From The Sky
I Am Ready to Succeed Not Try
If I Don't Invite You In
I Might Not Win
I Have Been Lost For Too Long
Help Me To Stay Strong

From

http://AngelRaphaelSpeaks.com/AAAAAAA/

25 - Private Channeling

Angel Raphael Speaks a series of free messages that are channeled through Reverend Mike Wanner for the Highest good and Highest Healing of all concerned.

Many questions arise about Reverend Mike doing private channeling, and he does help with that so e-mail him.

Reverend Mike is available worldwide as a psychic channel, emotional release facilitator, spiritual energy practitioner & teacher, and public speaker. He looks forward to meeting you soon!

Email - mikewann@voicenet.com 215-342-1270

PRIVATE SPIRITUAL READINGS/channelings or Spiritual Healing Sessions: Telephone or in person.

Rev. Mike is available for individual, intuitive one-on-one sessions with you, his Guide Family, and your Guides. He helps by offering clarity on emotional situations about your life, your purpose, your spirituality, and the release of stuffed emotions and cellular memory.

Connect to the love of your Guides today!

Contact Rev. Mike for an appointment.

Sessions available:

Spiritual Readings
Angel Channeling
Distant Reiki Healing
Distant Clearing of Stuffed Emotions
Distant Clearing Cellular Memory
Distant Clearing Energy Blockages
Distant Clearing of the Chakras
Customized needs
Mastermind dowsing responses to yes/no direction finding questions.

Rev. Mike is a facilitator of healing. He brings you and the Divine together so that you can align with the Divine and have a great time and a great life. All healing is between you and God, as it should be.

Go ahead and start without Rev. Mike. Visit his prayer site http://www.Create-A-Prayer.com. Take the first step NOW.

26 - Reverend Mike Wanner

Rev. Mike Wanner started his spiritual and ministerial studies with Reiki in 1993 and had studied seven styles of Reiki in the U.S., Japan, Canada, Denmark and Australia. He is certified to teach. He became certified to teach Integrated Energy Therapy in 1999 and co-taught the first IET class of the new Millennium. Mike began dowsing in 2001.

Ordained as a Metaphysical Minister of the International Metaphysical Ministry and an Interfaith Minister of the Circle of Miracles Ministry, Rev. Mike practices and teaches spiritual energy therapies in the Philadelphia Area.

Rev. Mike holds ministerial degrees from the University of Metaphysics and the University of Sedona. He is a Pastoral Care Associate at Jefferson - Aria - Frankford Hospital. He taught at the National Academy of Massage Therapy and Health Sciences.

Rev. Mike was a faculty member of the Medical Mission Sister's Center for Human Integration's School of Integrated Body/Mind Therapies in Fox Chase, Philadelphia, PA for twelve years.

Rev. Mike is licensed by the teaching of Intuitional Metaphysics to practice Spiritual Healing and Scientific Prayer. Mike is also a Prayer therapist.

Rev. Mike was elected in 2007 to the status of "Fellow of the American Institute of Stress."

In 2008, Rev. Mike became a practitioner of Coincidental Recognition as he incorporated the CoRe system into his spiritual healing practice.

In 2009, Rev. Mike trademarked a new healing process called Quantum Quatro! Subtle Energy System Support®.
In 2011, Rev. Mike joined the outreach program known as the Health Advantage Group.

In 2012, Rev. Mike became a Certified Professional Coach by The Master Coaching Academy and Joined The Personal Empowerment Group.

Prior to his spiritual, ministerial and coaching studies, Rev. Mike worked for Sears Roebuck and Co. while in High School and after graduation, until he joined the U. S. Air Force in 1965. He returned to Sears from Vietnam in 1969 and stayed until 1978. His final Sears assignment was as an efficiency expert in Methods - Operational Research and Development.

He volunteered with Burholme Emergency Medical Services from 1969 and is still a Life Member and Board of Directors Member. He started a private ambulance company in 1975 and worked professionally in the field until 2001 when he devoted his full attention to real estate investing, healing, coaching, and writing.

www.ReverendMikeWanner.com

www.ingramcontent.com/pod-product-compliance
Lightning Source LLC
Chambersburg PA
CBHW071158220526
45468CB00003B/1076